Spikes, Sc[ales] and Armor

Written by Jo Windsor

Rigby

Some animals have spikes. The spikes help to keep them safe.

This hedgehog has spikes.
When it rolls into a ball,
the spikes stick out.

3

This fish has spikes.
When it puffs up its body,
the spikes stick out.

This porcupine has spikes.
The spikes are very sharp.

Some animals have scales. The scales help to keep them safe.

6

This snake has scales on its body.
The scales are smooth so the snake can slide over the sand.

This armadillo has scales.
It can roll into a ball
to keep safe.

This pangolin can roll itself into a ball to keep safe, too.

Some animals have armor. The armor helps keep them safe.

This tortoise has a hard back.
It can pull in its legs and
its head to keep safe.

This snail has a hard back, too. It can stay inside the shell to keep safe.

12

This bird has armor on its head!
The armor keeps the bird's head safe.

People can put on things to keep safe, too.

Index

armadillo 8

bird 13

fish 4

hedgehog 3

pangolin 9

people 14

porcupine 5

snail 12

snake 7

tortoise 11

Guide Notes

Title: Spikes, Scales, and Armor
Stage: Early (3) – Blue

Genre: Nonfiction (Expository)
Approach: Guided Reading
Processes: Thinking Critically, Exploring Language, Processing Information
Visual Focus: Photographs (static images)

THINKING CRITICALLY
(sample questions)
- What do you think this book is going to tell us?
- What do you know about animals with spikes, scales, and armor?
- Focus the children's attention on the Index. Ask: "What animals are you going to find out about in this book?"
- If you want to find out about a hedgehog, what page would you look on?
- If you want to find out about a snake, what page would you look on?
- Look at pages 2 and 3. What special things do these animals have on their bodies?
- Look at pages 6 and 7. What do these animals have all over their bodies? Why do you think these animals have scales?
- Look at page 12. What does the snail do to keep safe?
- Look at page 14. How are the people keeping themselves safe?

EXPLORING LANGUAGE

Terminology
Title, cover, photographs, author, photographers

Vocabulary
Interest words: spikes, scales, armor, porcupine, pangolin, armadillo
High-frequency words (new): head, hard
Compound words: hedgehog, itself, into, inside

Print Conventions
Capital letter for sentence beginnings, periods, exclamation marks, commas